THE
CAHUILLA

by Craig A. Doherty and Katherine M. Doherty

Illustrated by Richard Smolinski

ROURKE PUBLICATIONS, INC.

VERO BEACH, FLORIDA 32964

CONTENTS

Printed in the USA

Library of Congress Cataloging-in-Publication Data

Doherty, Craig A.
    The Cahuilla / by Craig A. Doherty, Katherine M. Doherty.
        p. cm. — (Native American people)
        Includes bibliographical references.
        1. Cahuilla Indians—Juvenile literature. [1. Cahuilla Indians. 2. Indians of North America.]
    I. Doherty, Katherine M. II Title. III. Series.
    E99.C155D64 1994   978'.049745—dc20   93-31863
    ISBN 0-86625-527-3   CIP
                                                    AC

Introduction

For many years archaeologists—and other people who study early Native American cultures—agreed that the first humans to live in the Americas arrived about 11,500 years ago. These first Americans were believed to have been big-game hunters who lived by hunting the woolly mammoths and giant bison that inhabited the Ice Age plains of the Americas. This widely accepted theory also asserted that these first Americans crossed a land bridge linking Siberia, in Asia, to Alaska. This land bridge occurred when the accumulation of water in Ice Age glaciers lowered the level of the world's oceans.

In recent years, many scientists have challenged this theory. Although most agree that many big-game hunting bands left similar artifacts all over the Americas 11,500 years ago, many now suggest that the first Americans may have arrived as far back as 20,000 or even 50,000 years ago. There are those who think that some of these earliest Americans may have even come to the Americas by boat, working their way down the west coast of North America and South America.

In support of this theory, scientists who study language or genetics (the study of the inherited similarities and differences found in living things) believe that there may have been more than one period of migration. They

also believe that these multiple migrations started in different parts of Asia, which accounts for the genetic and language differences that exist among the people of the Americas. Although it is still not certain when the first Americans arrived, scientists agree that today's Native Americans are descendants of early Asian immigrants.

Over the thousands of years between the first arrivals from Asia and the introduction of Europeans, the people who were living in the Americas flourished and inhabited every corner of the two continents. Native Americans lived above the Arctic Circle in the North, to Tierra del Fuego at the tip of South America, and from the Atlantic Ocean in the East to the Pacific Ocean in the West.

The people of North America divided into hundreds of different groups. Each of these groups adapted to the environment in which it lived. As agriculture developed and spread throughout the Americas, some people switched from being nomads to living in one area. Along the Mississippi River, in the Southwest, in Mexico, and in Peru, groups of Native Americans built large cities. In other areas, groups continued to exist as hunters and gatherers with no permanent settlements.

Within the area that is now California, there may have been as many as 350,000 Native Americans before the arrival of the first Spanish explorers and settlers. These Native Americans belonged to a number of different tribes and adapted to the many ecological zones in the area. Today, 115 miles east of Los Angeles is the resort community of Palm Springs. This area is also home to the Cahuilla.

Origins of the Cahuilla

Archaeologists believe that the first nomadic hunters and gatherers came from the north between 2,000 and 3,000 years ago. They arrived at a vast lake in the southern desert of what is now California. It was called Lake Cahuilla and was probably formed when the northern reaches of the Sea of Cortez were cut off by shifting sands. Lake Cahuilla dried up before the coming of Europeans. During the early 1900s, floodwaters from the Colorado River formed the Salton Sea in the same location.

Archaeological evidence indicates the earliest Cahuilla people ate fish, shellfish, and water plants from the lake. As the lake dried up, they adapted to the desert, learning how to use a variety of plants and animals. Although the Cahuilla lived in the desert of southern California, archaeologists have found evidence that they traded with many other tribes throughout a wide area.

The Cahuilla language is part of the Uto-Aztecan family of Native American languages. The Uto-Aztecan language group includes the Aztecs and Toltecs of Mexico and the Ute and Paiute of Colorado and Utah. Tribes within one language group could usually understand the dialect of a nearby tribe but were not able to understand the language of a tribe that was far away.

Daily Life

Different climates and situations call for different types of housing. The Cahuilla needed to protect themselves from the strong winds of the desert. Water was also a primary concern. Therefore, most Cahuilla villages were located in the canyons of the area. Here, springs provided them with water, while canyons protected them from the winds. In addition to the variety of shelters the Cahuilla built, they also used the natural caves that were found in the canyons they inhabited. The caves were cool in the summer and easy to heat in the winter.

The smallest types of shelters they built were made of brush and were only big enough for four people to crawl into and sleep. The Cahuilla also built dome-shaped and rectangular-shaped houses that were between fifteen and twenty feet long. These larger houses had a pole frame and were thatched with a variety of plants. Palm fronds, tule reeds, and arrowweed were all used as building materials. Occasionally, the Cahuilla also coated the thatched walls with adobe mud. A hole was left in the highest point of each roof to let smoke from their fires escape.

This ceremonial house, or **Kish úmnowwit,** *is the last one in existence in Palm Springs, California. Francisco Patencio, an important village leader, is shown outside of the dwelling.*

In addition to the shelters they built, the Cahuilla used natural caves as dwellings.

In some Cahuilla villages a group of closely related families would connect their houses by building roofed walkways to provide shade. Sometimes these walkways had one wall to shield the families from the wind.

A larger ceremonial house was built using the same pole-and-thatch construction as some smaller buildings. The home of the *net*, the Cahuilla village leader, was generally bigger than most and usually located next to the ceremonial building.

Throughout the year, the Cahuilla spent time in other parts of their large territory gathering food and hunting. Temporary shelters, consisting mainly of brush shelters, were often constructed at these sites.

Family Life

Among the Cahuilla, the family was important. A strong and large family working together was necessary to meet the needs of all the family members. In the Cahuilla language there are sixty-five different words to define relatives. The Cahuilla were very exact in defining relationships. One of their rules was that you could not marry a person who was related to you as far back as five generations. This made it important to keep careful track not only of all your living relatives, but also at least five generations of your ancestors.

When a Cahuilla marriage took place it was usually arranged by the parents of the intended bride and groom. In order to find husbands and wives who were not related through the last five generations, the bride and groom's families were often from villages as far apart as fifty miles. When the Cahuilla married, young women moved and became part of their husband's family. A groom's family would give a bride's family many gifts. This was in part to compensate them for the loss of their daughter. Cahuilla women usually married at the age of twelve or thirteen; the young men were usually four or five years older. When two people married, their families considered themselves joined together.

The two families would often work to help each other. A young woman was expected to immediately begin helping her husband's family with the never-ending task of collecting and preparing food. A newly married husband was expected to provide a share of the meat that the extended family needed.

As soon as they were able, Cahuilla children began learning the skills they needed to be successful members of the community. The smallest children were allowed to play all day long, but by the time they were eight or nine years old, their education became more important than play. Like many Native American groups, the Cahuilla taught their children skills by having them help out. Young boys watched their older male relatives make tools and hunting equipment. During this time, both boys and girls might also be told stories that would instruct them in the ways of the tribe.

Cahuilla girls were raised to leave their families and go to the homes of their husbands' families. They were put in charge of the youngest children in order to learn about motherly duties. Girls also helped with the collecting and preparing of food. Since girls were often married at twelve or thirteen, they had a lot to learn in a relatively short period of time.

Food

Within the Cahuilla territory were four distinct ecozones. The Cahuilla villages were located in what scientists call the Lower Sonoran Zone. This is the low desert, where many different types of cactus, yucca, and mesquite are the main types of plants. Above 3,500 feet in elevation the land becomes the Upper Sonoran Zone,

characterized by piñon pine, juniper, and some oak trees. Above 6,300 feet is the Transition Zone, which has a variety of large evergreen trees and stands of oak. The final zone in their territory is the Canadian-Hudsonian Zone, which is above 9,000 feet. This is an alpine area that offers some hunting opportunities in the warmer months, but very little in the way of plant food.

From these different zones the Cahuilla collected blossoms, leaves, bark, fruit, and seeds from over 300 different plants. Most of the food gathering was done by women and children, although men helped during times of major harvesting. Secondary to the harvesting of wild plants, the Cahuilla practiced agriculture. In their fields they grew corn, squash, melons, and beans. The Cahuilla also tended the wild plants that they harvested, pruning them to encourage growth. They also watered certain wild plants during times of drought.

The most important food that the Cahuilla gathered was the acorn. It is believed that the Cahuilla used the acorns from six different varieties of oak trees. The acorn harvest, the busiest time of year for the Cahuilla, usually lasted for two to three weeks in the fall. During this time, they moved up into the oak groves that were found in both the Upper Sonoran and Transition zones. The men would climb up into the trees and shake the branches while the women and children picked up the acorns. Sometimes the women processed the acorns at the collecting site.

As many acorns as possible were shelled, so that they would be lighter

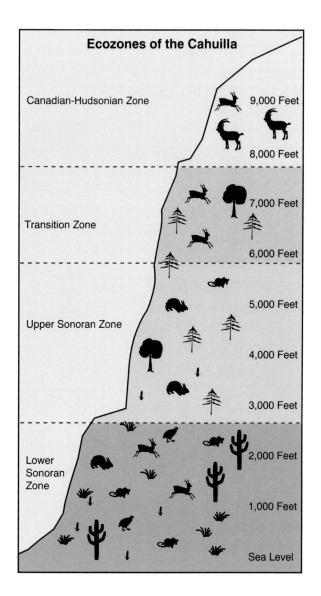

Ecozones of the Cahuilla

Canadian-Hudsonian Zone   9,000 Feet

8,000 Feet

Transition Zone   7,000 Feet

6,000 Feet

Upper Sonoran Zone   5,000 Feet

4,000 Feet

3,000 Feet

Lower Sonoran Zone   2,000 Feet

1,000 Feet

Sea Level

Gathering acorns was an important task. Cahuilla men climbed trees to shake the acorns to the ground, and the women and children collected them.

to carry. They also had to be crushed and leached before they could be used. Acorns are very bitter-tasting, because they contain a chemical called tannin. The tannin was leached out of the acorn meal by pouring hot water over it and then allowing the water to drain. The Cahuilla used large pack baskets to transport the acorns and acorn meal back to their villages. Some of these baskets were even big enough to carry as much as one hundred pounds of acorns.

Once all of the acorns had been processed and properly dried, the acorn meal had to be safely stored. The Cahuilla men built raised granaries for storing acorn meal and other nuts

Raised storage baskets were used by the Cahuilla to protect food from animals.

and grains. The granaries were raised a few feet off the ground to keep out rodents. Willow twigs were used to make the basketlike container that was three to five feet in diameter and approximately three feet deep. When the granary was covered and sealed with pine pitch, acorn meal would keep for several years. The Cahuilla also stored food in pottery containers and baskets, which were then put in caves near their villages.

Piñon nuts, various cactus fruits, mesquite blossoms, and seed pods, plus numerous roots, berries, grass, and other seeds were also used by the Cahuilla. Piñon nuts were a valued,

although not always dependable crop, which provided a very concentrated food of over 3,000 calories per pound. Mesquite of two varieties, the honey mesquite and the screwbean, also produced great quantities of food. Mesquite blossoms were roasted and mixed with water to create a beverage, while the seed pods were eaten both fresh and dried. The beans were either cooked whole or were ground into a flour that could be stored and used later.

With so many available plant foods, the Cahuilla diet was extremely varied. Porridges, soups, and stews were made with an endless array of ingredients.

These meals were often cooked in baskets, by taking hot rocks from the fire and adding them to the liquid. Clay pots, another option for cooking, were put directly over the fire. The Cahuilla also ate many different types of seed cakes and used acorn meal to make a kind of pancake.

The women made many of their own kitchen utensils, including the baskets and pottery items. Utensils of wood or stone were usually made by the men. One very important set of tools in a Cahuilla kitchen was the *mano* and *metate*. The *metate* was a large, flat stone, and the *mano* was a smaller stone that could be held in the hand. Seeds, nuts, or corn were placed directly on the *metate* and then ground with the *mano*. Reportedly, a woman's skill as a cook was often judged by how finely she could grind her flour.

A Cahuilla woman grinding cornmeal in a stone mortar in 1897.

Hunting

The Cahuilla territory also supported an abundance of animal life. Very few animals were not included in the Cahuilla diet. Everything from insects, such as ants and grasshoppers, to rattlesnakes and other reptiles found their way onto the menu. Mammals from the smallest rodent to deer, antelope, and mountain sheep were also hunted for food.

The Cahuilla had almost as many hunting techniques as they had game to hunt. Nets, snares, pit traps, clubs, fire, throwing sticks, and bows and arrows were all used to capture game.

Deer were often stalked by a single Cahuilla hunter who camouflaged himself by wearing a deer hide and antlers. Dressed as a deer, a hunter could get very close and then shoot with his bow. The Cahuilla hunters sometimes put the venom of black widow spiders or rattlesnakes onto their arrowheads. The poison did not kill the animals, but it made it easier for the hunters to catch up to and finish off wounded animals.

Pronghorn antelope were difficult to hunt, due to their excellent vision and their tendency to stay out in the open where they are able to spot any danger. Antelope can also run at speeds approaching sixty miles per hour. However, antelope do not have a lot of endurance, so Cahuilla hunters would set up relay teams to chase them. In this way, the antelope soon became exhausted and the hunters were able to get close enough to kill them.

Mountain sheep stayed in the highest and least accessible elevations of the Cahuilla territory. To hunt them, Cahuilla men built brush blinds near water holes that were being used by mountain sheep. They then hid in the blinds and waited in hopes that one of the animals would pass close enough to shoot it with an arrow.

Although large animals were prized for their meat, hides, and other usable parts, smaller animals provided most of the meat that the Cahuilla ate. This was due to the fact that the smaller animals were plentiful and more easily found close to the Cahuilla villages. Many small animals and birds were killed with a throwing stick, which was a couple of feet long and curved up at one end. The Cahuilla hunters were very accurate with their throwing sticks.

One Cahuilla delicacy was quail. A quail was prepared by encasing it in wet clay and then placing it in the fire. After the clay ball hardened it was removed from the fire. When it was split open, a juicy, fully cooked quail was ready to eat.

The men were usually responsible for butchering and skinning the animals they killed. Meat, often roasted over an open fire, was also added to stews and soups. When larger animals were killed, any meat that was not going to be eaten quickly was dried and stored for later use. The Cahuilla wasted very little.

When a large amount of meat was needed for a ceremonial feast or other important occasion, everyone in the village would join in a community hunt. Large numbers of small animals,

Opposite: Cahuilla hunters learned to hide quietly and wait for mountain sheep to come close enough to be able to hit them with their arrows.

Opposite: A Cahuilla hunter cleverly disguises himself in order to stalk a deer.

especially rabbits, would be captured as a long line of people moved across a field.

One of a hunter's most important possessions was his bow. Cahuilla bows were made using either willow or mesquite wood. They were strung with either sinew (tendons) or a string made of the fibers of the mescal plant. Their arrows varied depending on the task, but many were made from cane or arrowweed, with either wooden or stone arrowheads. The arrows were finished with three feathers tied on with sinew.

In addition to his bow, each hunter had a special stone that was used for straightening arrow shafts. This straightening stone, made of soapstone, had a groove cut into it. To straighten an arrow shaft, the stone was heated. The hunter would then dampen the shaft and slide it back and forth in the groove until the arrow was straight.

These stones were marked with certain designs that the Cahuilla believed to be magical. The knowledge of the bow and arrow and the straightening stone was thought to have been given to the Cahuilla people by their creator god, *Mukat*.

Arts and Crafts

Members of the Cahuilla tribe basically practiced two major art forms, rock art and basket weaving. Archaeologists believe that the practice of creating pictures on rocks began about 1,000 years ago.

The Cahuilla created two different types of images on rock faces in their territory—pictographs and petroglyphs. A pictograph is an image painted on the rocks. The Cahuilla used a number of different-colored minerals and charcoal to make several colors. Once these substances were finely ground, they were mixed with animal fat to make the paint. A petroglyph is created by chipping away the darker rock, and revealing the lighter stone underneath. A piece of a much harder stone was used as a tool to chip away at the soft, sandstone rock face.

Scientists believe that, originally, rock art may have been used to mark the boundaries of the Cahuilla territory. Later designs seem to illustrate images of religious importance or significant historical events.

In addition to their beautiful rock art, the Cahuilla people have also created intricate baskets. The women of the tribe have always been excellent basket makers, fashioning coil baskets in a wide variety of shapes and sizes and weaving geometric designs and symbols of religious importance into them. Most of the traditional Cahuilla baskets were made using a variety of local grasses. Some of the grasses were dyed black, unless darker-colored grasses were available to be used for a design.

Flat baskets were used as plates and for collecting and winnowing seeds. Both shallow and deep baskets that had flat bottoms filled a number of needs. The largest baskets that the Cahuilla women made were the cone-shaped pack baskets that were so important for carrying gathered food back to the village.

Top: Cahuilla artists created beautiful rock art called pictographs. Left: A Cahuilla woman, Maria Casseuv, works on the flat section of a coiled basket.

Political and Social Organization

The Cahuilla had a complete political and social organization. Everyone in the tribe belonged to one of two groups called moieties. One moiety was symbolized by the coyote, the other by the cougar. In the Cahuilla language the coyote is called *ʔistam* (the *ʔ* sounds like a gulp) and the cougar is called *tuktem*. There were a number of clans within each moiety, and as many as ten family groups, or lineages, within each clan.

One's position within the social structure of the Cahuilla tribe was determined at birth. A Cahuilla child automatically became a member of the father's family, clan, and moiety. When it was time to marry, Cahuilla always married someone from the other moiety. A Coyote had to marry a Cougar, and vice versa.

The political and ceremonial leaders of the Cahuilla were called *nets*. The *net* was the hereditary male leader of a family group, assisted in his duties by a *paxa*, who was responsible for making sure that all religious obligations were fulfilled by the community. The *net*, with the advice of the *paxa*, directed most of the activities of the group. It was his responsibility to schedule the harvesting of foods at the proper time, as well as oversee the community's lands.

Although the Cahuilla did not own land individually, their territory was divided and marked. Each community had a set territory, and the lands farther away were also divided among the clans. One clan might have the rights to over 600 square miles. The boundaries were always clearly marked with petroglyphs, piles of stones, and natural features of the land.

The *net* was the head of the community, but he did not rule alone. The Cahuilla, like many Native American groups, needed to be in agreement before making major decisions. The *net* would consult with the older members of the community to determine what was best for everyone. The Cahuilla believed that the longer people live the more wisdom they obtain, and they were very respectful of the opinions of the community elders.

Francisco Patencio, shown here with his wife Dolores, was the last ceremonial leader, or net, *of the Agua Caliente band of Cahuilla in Palm Springs, California.*

Religious Life

In modern times, religion is a separate part of many people's lives, but for the Cahuilla it was an integral part of everything they did. They strongly believed that their world was closely related to the spiritual world. Because of this, proper respect was always paid

to the spirit world in the Cahuilla's daily tasks, as well as during important ceremonial events.

The Cahuilla believed that the world and all that is in it was created by *Mukat* and *Temayawut*. Legends told that in the beginning there was darkness, until colors swirled together. As the colors met at one point, these two

The Cahuilla believed that **Temayawut** *(left), and* **Mukat** *(right), were supernatural twins who were responsible for creating life.*

twin supernatural beings were created. After their birth, they began to create the world and its inhabitants. *Mukat* worked slowly and carefully, using black mud. *Temayawut* worked quickly and without care, using white mud.

When they were finished, *Mukat* had a few excellently crafted beings, while *Temayawut* had many crudely fashioned beings. They fought over whose beings should live and whose should die. *Temayawut* finally took his creatures and left. *Mukat's* creatures came to life, and when the sun came up they were frightened and all began to talk in different languages. *Mukat* could understand only the man who spoke the Cahuilla language, and that man was to be the first Cahuilla.

Within the Cahuilla community were a number of different religious roles. The *paxa* was responsible for making sure that the everyday activities of the *net* and the community adhered to religious rules. The person who was the Cahuilla equivalent of a minister, priest, or rabbi was called the *shaman,* or *puul.*

The *puul* officiated at the many ceremonies that the Cahuilla held during the year. He was also believed to be able to cure people who were sick or injured.

Two other religious positions were important among the Cahuilla. Some men became *hauniks,* or ritual singers. In a culture with no written records of its rituals or history, it was important to have members of the community who could memorize huge quantities of information and recite it when needed. Some of the songs that the Cahuilla *hauniks* had to learn took up to twelve hours to sing. The other important religious role was that of *ngengewish,* or ritual dancer. These men would learn the dances that were a part of the frequent Cahuilla religious ceremonies.

Many events within the lives of the Cahuilla were marked with rituals. Birth and death were observed to remind the Cahuilla of their close connection with the spirit world. The first harvest of acorns or mesquite in a year was also marked by a ceremony, as were a hunter's first deer, antelope, or mountain sheep.

When children reached the age of five, a naming ceremony was held. All the boys and girls of a family group,

along with their family members, and the religious leaders, would assemble in the ceremonial house. The families of the children being named always brought plenty of food to share with their relatives. So much food was needed for the celebration that some children had to wait to receive their names, while their families stored up enough food for the naming feast. After the feast and ritual songs and dances, the *net* would give each child his or her official name. A child was usually given a name that belonged to a past relative but was not being used by any living relative. Girls were often given names that related to flowers and plants. Boys' names typically had something to do with animals or insects.

One of the most important ceremonies for a Cahuilla was initiation into the tribe. This occurred at age twelve or thirteen and signified the transition into adulthood. Boys and girls went through initiation separately. All boys in a family group of appropriate age were initiated together. The initiation might take a few days, or more likely a few weeks. During this time, boys were not allowed to eat much and had to perform feats of great physical exertion, such as running great distances. Many of the spiritual secrets and responsibilities of the Cahuilla were revealed to the boys at this initiation time. This was also when boys were tattooed and had their noses and ears pierced so that they could wear the traditional ornaments of a Cahuilla man.

Opposite: Running long distances was one of the tasks that Cahuilla boys accomplished during their initiation ceremonies.

A Cahuilla girl always went through initiation alone after her first menstruation. During a girl's initiation, a pit was dug in the center of the ceremonial house, or somewhere nearby, and a fire was built in the pit. When the fire died down, the ashes and hot coals were removed and the pit was lined with grasses and herbs. A Cahuilla girl would then climb down into the pit and her body would be covered with more herbs and furs. She would stay in the pit from three to five days while the *haunik* taught her the songs of her clan. A Cahuilla girl only left the pit when it needed to be reheated.

Cahuilla girls did not have to fast as the boys did, but could only eat lightly during their initiations. Girls were often married shortly after their initiations.

Clothing

Due to the mild desert climate of the Cahuilla territory, clothing was very simple. The men wore loincloths and either hide shoes or sandals. The women wore skirts and sandals. The women's skirts were made of skins or woven from strips of bark or other plant fibers.

The fibers of the mescal plant were soaked in mud before they were used to make skirts and sandals. This process whitened the fibers. Sandals were tied on using either fiber or deerskin laces. Baby diapers were made from the bark of mesquite trees. In colder weather, a blanket that was made from strips of rabbit fur woven together was worn.

Opposite: A Cahuilla girl was covered with herbs and furs in her ceremonial initiation pit. Right: A Cahuilla woman and man in traditional dress.

23

Cahuilla men enjoyed playing a game of **shinny**.

Games

Games are an important part of any culture, and the Cahuilla engaged in a number of them. Children often played with tops and jacks. They also played a game called *shinny*, in which two teams would line up to face each other, with two posts set up at either end of the lines to serve as goals. The object of the game was to kick a ball through the opponent's goal without leaving the line. The Cahuilla also enjoyed juggling.

Footraces were a major activity for both men and women. The only way to get from one place to another, before the horse was introduced by the Spanish, was on foot. Being able to cover great distances quickly was an important skill for the Cahuilla. The boys also played at the skills they would need to become good hunters. Archery contests were a popular activity.

No matter what the game was, the Cahuilla often enjoyed gambling on it. Baskets, tools, and other possessions were wagered.

European Contact

Columbus made the first European contact with Native Americans of the Caribbean in 1492. Nearly 130 years later, the Pilgrims landed at Plymouth Rock in 1620. In 1680, the Pueblo of New Mexico revolted and drove the Spanish out of their territory for a time. And in 1776, the Declaration of Independence was signed in the city of Philadelphia, just two years after the first European, Juan Bautista de Anza, visited the lands of the Cahuilla.

The Spanish had established control of the Aztec lands in 1522, and had spread north and south from there. In the middle of the eighteenth century, the Spanish became concerned that the

British and Russians would take over the lands they claimed in California. To prevent this, they began building missions along the coast. The first mission, in what is now California, was at San Diego in 1769. The coastal tribes were forced to work for this mission and to become Catholics. The Cahuilla were not directly affected by the Spanish settlements because of their isolation in the desert.

The Cahuilla were probably exposed to the diseases of the Europeans by interactions with other Native Americans who had contracted the diseases. At first, the Cahuilla had no direct contact with the Spanish, although they were aware of them from trading with the coastal tribes. By the early 1800s, the Spanish had set up missions away from the coast at San Bernadino, San Ysabel, and Pala. These missions were much nearer to the Cahuilla territory. Mission records show that as early as 1809, there were a few Cahuilla who had been baptized as Catholics. At this point in time, it has been estimated that there were more than 30,000 Cahuilla.

The missions established farms and ranches to support themselves, and the Native Americans of California were quick to adapt to this new agriculture and ranching. A few Cahuilla lived at the San Bernadino mission and learned these new ways. The Spanish cattle herds began to spill over onto Cahuilla territory at this time.

The Mexican Revolution began in 1810, and in 1822, the Mexicans finally succeeded in defeating the Spanish. This brought about many changes in California. Mexican officials were interested in gaining more territory and exploring the inland areas of California. Until this time, contact between Mexico and California had only been made by ship. Then, the Mexican Captain Jose Romero laid out an overland route from Arizona to California that went right through the heart of Cahuilla territory. This route depended on the hot springs at Agua Caliente, now called Palm Springs. During this time, the Mexicans took over more and more Cahuilla lands for ranching and farming.

By the middle of the nineteenth century, the Cahuilla were living in peace with their Mexican neighbors. Many of the Cahuilla even worked as laborers on Mexican ranches. A number of them moved to the property of Antonio Maria Lugo and his sons to help them work and protect the 37,000-acre Lugo ranch. At this time, bands of Ute from the East had taken to raiding the ranches of California for horses and other livestock.

Just when the Cahuilla and other California tribes had learned to get along with the Mexicans who were in California, the situation changed again. In 1848, the United States won a war with Mexico and took over what is today New Mexico, Arizona, and California.

The attempts of the United States to deal with the Native Americans of California were flawed from the beginning. Many whites were accused of cheating the government on food orders for the Native Americans. The government set up one 50,000-acre reservation for approximately 2,000 Native Americans and left the other 60,000-plus Native Americans on their own. Fortunately for the Cahuilla,

*Juan Bautista de Anza was the
first European to visit the Cahuilla.*

By 1885, many Cahuilla had moved to Antonio Maria Lugo's ranch for work and to help protect the property from Ute raids.

they were able to survive in their traditional manner with little interference from the government. At this point, no one had found a use for the desert lands they inhabited. Otherwise, they too would have been subjected to the destruction of their way of life, as so many Native Americans in California experienced at this time.

In 1862 and 1863, the Cahuilla suffered through a smallpox epidemic that reduced their population to approximately 2,500 people. By this time, it was hard to fight the pressure from the growing non-Indian population. In 1877, reservations were established for the Cahuilla that greatly reduced their territory. For a while, the Cahuilla were allowed to live without too much interference on these reservations. In 1891, however, the U.S. government took a more active role in supervising the Cahuilla. Government schools were set up, and Protestant missionaries were encouraged to work among the Cahuilla. The objective of U.S. Indian policy at this time was to make Native Americans part of mainstream culture.

The Cahuilla were able to withstand these first attacks on their culture. Then the government divided the reservations up into small allotments that made it almost impossible for the Cahuilla to continue their traditional lifestyle. Life for the Cahuilla, like for most reservation residents of the time, became a matter of dependence on the federal government.

In 1934, the federal government passed the Indian Reorganization Act, which gave the Cahuilla more control running their own reservations. A great amount of damage had already been done, however, and the Cahuilla continued to face hardships economically, as well as in the areas of public health and education.

The Cahuilla Today

According to the 1990 U.S. Census, there are 1,418 Cahuilla today and most of them live in southern California. A number of Cahuilla live off the reservations but still nearby, because of the lack of adequate housing and services on the reservations. The prosperity of the surviving Cahuilla varies greatly. Some of the Cahuilla who have allotments of land on the Agua Caliente Reservation have

become wealthy. The 25,000-plus acres of the Agua Caliente are situated in the middle of Palm Springs. Much of this land is leased to the city and independent developers.

The Agua Caliente Cahuilla are in the process of planning and building a casino that will be operated by Caesar's Palace. Smaller gambling ventures exist on some of the more rural Cahuilla reservations. On the 25,000-acre Los Coyotes Reservation, where only twenty Cahuilla live, a park for mobile homes has been developed. As a means of making money, the Cahuilla have also leased approximately 500 acres of reservation land of Los Coyotes to a company that is planning to use it for a solid-waste disposal site.

Many of the Cahuilla rituals and traditions have been lost, and much of the language forgotten. Fortunately, attempts are now being made to save what is left of traditional Cahuilla culture. The Malki Museum on the Morongo Reservation has been established as a place to preserve and display Cahuilla artifacts. Language classes are also offered in an attempt to keep the language alive. Also, every Memorial Day weekend a *fiesta*, or party, is held to celebrate Cahuilla culture.

Some of the traditional Cahuilla ceremonies are remembered and are now performed in English. The majority of the Cahuilla people are Catholics, and a few are Protestants. Some Cahuilla still gather traditional foods, but usually only in very small quantities for special occasions.

The future of the Cahuilla is quite uncertain. As the Palm Springs area continues to be built up, the pressure on the Cahuilla to give up more and

European contact affected different aspects of Native American culture, including the style of dress that many Native Americans eventually adopted.

more of their lands for development will be hard to resist. Although the sale of Cahuilla lands may mean prosperity, it also removes the Cahuilla from one of their most important links with their cultural past—the land. In the face of all this, many Cahuilla are determined that they will be able to maintain their unique identity as a people and face whatever challenges are ahead.

Chronology

1522   The Spanish take control of the Aztec lands.

1680   The Pueblo of New Mexico drive the Spanish out of their territory.

1769   The first mission in what is now San Diego is established.

1774   Juan Bautista de Anza is the first European to make contact with the Cahuilla.

1809   Members of the Cahuilla tribe are baptized at the Catholic mission at San Bernadino.

1810   The Mexican Revolution begins.

1822   Mexicans defeat the Spanish and declare independence. Mexican policy in California puts pressure on Native Americans for land.

1848   Treaty of Guadalupe Hidalgo ends the Mexican-American War and gives the United States the lands that become the states of Colorado, New Mexico, Arizona, California, Nevada, and Utah.

1862–1863   Smallpox epidemic among the Cahuilla reduces their population to approximately 2,500 people.

1877   The U.S. government sets up reservations for the Cahuilla, greatly reducing their traditional territory.

1891   U.S. Indian policy changes and the federal government begins to take an active role in trying to bring Native Americans into the mainstream of American culture.

1934   Indian Reorganization Act passes in the U.S. Congress and gives the Cahuilla, and all Native Americans living on reservations, more local control.

INDEX

Acknowledgments and Photo Credits
Cover and all artwork by Richard Smolinski.
Pages 5, 17: Courtesy of the Agua Caliente Cultural Museum; pp. 10, 11, 16, 30:
Smithsonian Institution/National Anthropological Archives; p. 28: Courtesy California
Historical Society, Los Angeles.
Map and chart by Blackbirch Graphics, Inc.